S0-AHH-113

Seals

by Martha E. H. Rustad

Consulting Editor: Gail Saunders-Smith, Ph.D.

Consultant: Jody Byrum, Science Writer,
SeaWorld Education Department

Pebble Books

an imprint of Capstone Press
Mankato, Minnesota

Pebble Books are published by Capstone Press
151 Good Counsel Drive, P.O. Box 669, Mankato, Minnesota 56002
http://www.capstone-press.com

Copyright © 2001 Capstone Press. All rights reserved.
No part of this book may be reproduced without written permission
from the publisher. The publisher takes no responsibility for the use of any
of the materials or methods described in this book, nor for the products thereof.
Printed in the United States of America.

2 3 4 5 6 06 05 04 03 02

Library of Congress Cataloging-in-Publication Data
Rustad, Martha E. H. (Martha Elizabeth Hillman), 1975–
  Seals / by Martha E. H. Rustad.
  p. cm.—(Ocean life)
  Includes bibliographical references (p. 23) and index.
  ISBN 0-7368-0860-4
  1. Seals (Animals)—Juvenile literature. [1. Seals (Animals)] I. Title. II. Series.
QL737.P6 R87 2001
599.79—dc21

00-009863

Summary: Simple text and photographs present seals and their behavior.

Note to Parents and Teachers

The Ocean Life series supports national science standards for units
on the diversity and unity of life. The series shows that animals
have features that help them live in different environments. This
book describes seals and illustrates how they live. The photographs
support early readers in understanding the text. The repetition of
words and phrases helps early readers learn new words. This book
also introduces early readers to subject-specific vocabulary words,
which are defined in the Words to Know section. Early readers may
need assistance to read some words and to use the Table of
Contents, Words to Know, Read More, Internet Sites, and
Index/Word List sections of the book.

Table of Contents

Seals are mammals.

Seals live in
and near oceans.

Seals have a nose
and whiskers.

flipper

Seals have four flippers.

Seals have fur.

Seals have fat
called blubber.

16

Seals have sharp teeth.

18

Most seals eat fish.

Seals can dive deep into the ocean.

Words to Know

blubber—fat under the skin of some animals

dive—to plunge deeply underwater; some seals can dive up to 6,000 feet (1,800 meters) below the surface of the ocean; they can stay underwater for 1 hour or more.

fish—a cold-blooded animal that lives in water and has scales, fins, and gills; seals eat fish as well as squid, penguin, crab, and shrimp.

flipper—a flat limb with bones on a sea animal; flippers help seals swim.

mammal—a warm-blooded animal with a backbone; mammals feed milk to their young.

ocean—a large body of salt water; seals live in the ocean but go onto land to rest, mate, and raise young.

teeth—the hard, white mouthparts used to bite food; seals grab food with their teeth, but they do not chew their food.

whisker—a long, stiff hair near the mouth of some animals; seals use whiskers to feel.

Read More

Piasetsky, Lome. *Fur Seals and Other Pinnipeds.*
Animals of the World. Chicago: World Book, 2000.

Staub, Frank J. *Sea Lions.* Early Bird Nature Books.
Minneapolis: Lerner Publications, 2000.

Woodward, John. *Seals.* Endangered! New York:
Benchmark Books, 1997.

Internet Sites

Harbor Seals
http://seaworld.org/infobooks/HarborSeal/
home.html

Pinniped Photo Gallery
http://nmml.afsc.noaa.gov/gallery/pinnipeds.htm

The Pinnipeds
http://www.marinemammalcenter.org/learning/
education/pinnipeds/pinnipeds.asp

Seals and Sea Lions
http://www.photolib.noaa.gov/animals/seals1.html   23

Index/Word List

Word Count: 42
Early-Intervention Level: 7

Credits
Steve Christensen, cover designer and illustrator; Kia Bielke, production designer;
    Kimberly Danger, photo researcher

Corel Corporation, 8, 12
François Gohier, 10
Jay Ireland & Georgienne E. Bradley, cover, 1, 4, 20
Joe McDonald, 16
Robin Brandt, 6, 14
William B. Folsom, 18